Worksheets Plus

Year 4

Book 3

Solving Problems

Covering:
Making Decisions and
Checking Results,
Money and Real Life Problems,
Reasoning About Shapes and Numbers

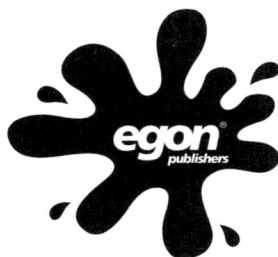

egon
publishers

EGON PUBLISHERS LTD • BALDOCK • ENGLAND

Worksheets Plus
Year 4, Book 3
Solving Problems
Authors: Steve Chinn, Julie Kay and Les Skidmore

ISBN: 1 899998 61 6

Published in 2001
by Egon Publishers Ltd
Royston Road, Baldock,
Herts SG7 6NW

Typeset by Partners in Style, Berkhamsted, Herts HP4 3HZ

Printed by Streets Printers, Royston Road, Baldock, Herts SG7 6NW

Year 4

Teaching guidance

These guide lines are just that. They are only meant to offer basic guidance with some emphasis on high-lighting potential areas of difficulty so that as many of these as possible can be pre-empted.

If you want more detailed ideas on teaching time table facts or addition and subtraction, then Egon publishes the 'What to do when you can't' . . . . . series. The third book (on multiplication and division) is in preparation.

For low stress overview of numeracy, see "Sum Hope, Breaking the Numbers Barrier" written by Steve Chinn and published by Souvenir Press.

The work in Year 4 is significantly less demanding than the work in Year 5. The development towards Year 5 work must be born in mind as you teach this syllabus. The programme sets in place many fundamental ideas and facts. The more secure and internalised this knowledge is, the more likely development will continue. The basic understanding of numbers and operations is a vital part of the Year 4 programme.

Solving problems

Making decisions

Making up 'number stories' is an important activity. Too often teachers expect pupils to 'translate' word problems into mathematical equations/statements whilst forgetting the reverse translation. By doing this pupils can learn how word problems are constructed and how misleading features can be introduced, such as extraneous data. It can also be fun and creative! Making up number stories can help pupils understand how key words can be used to mean different operations and move them away from an overly literal interpretation of vocabulary.

Identifying the operation in questions such as $52 * 5 = 260$ introduces another estimation sub-skill and teaches pupils another way to evaluate the answer by considering if it will be bigger, smaller, the same and how much bigger or smaller.

Reasoning about numbers and shapes

It is not always easy for a pupil to explain their reasoning for a mental calculation. Some pupils may find that their method is so intuitive (and quick) that they cannot easily explain all that happened in their brain. This may improve as pupils become accustomed to the idea of analysing their thinking.

Pupils' methods are not always the most efficient (though this judgment can be subjective) or consistent. Of course, once a teacher knows the procedure used by a pupil, she or he might be tempted to suggest changes or alternatives. This may not always be the best move and adopting a new procedure may take considerable time and practise for the pupil. This whole area of processing numbers (cognitive style) is fascinating and important. Ideally pupils should learn to be flexible in their choice of methods (and, hopefully appropriate to their own sub-skills), being able to use successfully a range of procedures. For most pupils this will happen over a period of time of exposure to the idea and encouragement to work in this more open manner (For more details on cognitive style see "Mathematics for Dyslexics: A Teaching handbook" by Chinn and Ashcroft, published by Whurr. Cognitive style is not just something to consider for dyslexic pupils, it is a factor for ALL pupils).

This topic area can be used to develop further flexibility in using numbers and to show the inter-relationships, especially those which make the manipulation of numbers easier, for example rounding 8s and 9s to tens, adjusting differences (46 - 28 adjusted to 48 - 28), adding through tens and hundreds for subtractions. All these techniques require that the pupil's first reaction is to appraise ALL the numbers in the question. There is a balance between the mathematical culture of answering quickly and the need to overview before computing.

Spatial examples can be a break from number crunching activities and may well allow some pupils who have strong spatial skills to succeed.

Unstructured questions (for example ▼ + ❋ + ▶ = 1) will be very challenging for some pupils. Some will just not have the confidence or skill to actually start the process, even with encouragement. Be prepared to lead more than you might want!

Problems involving 'real life', money and measure

The Numeracy Strategy provides ample opportunity for reviews, revisits and revision. This overlearning is a strong positive factor in the acquisition of numeracy skills. Additionally, the interlinking of different sections can be used to help develop and consolidate concepts. So word problems occur again giving another chance to explore the meaning and uses of mathematical vocabulary.

This section allows teachers to introduce some truly 'real life' work, such as money and measures. It would seem an ideal section in which to use manipulative materials such as coins, bottles, scales and such. Let pupils experience quantities such as 100g, 100ml and see everyday recognisable examples to give them real benchmark values to use as a basis for judging their answers in this area.

When dealing with questions based on recipes, talk about the reality of proportions which lead to, say 5 1/2 eggs.

With questions on time, remind pupils that for time 60 and 12 are key numbers. Practise counting through a minute and an hour (58 seconds, 59 seconds, 60 seconds which is 1 minute, 1 minute and 1 second .... Similarly 58 minutes, 59 minutes, 60 minutes which is 1 hour. 1 hour and 1 minute ......).

Bridging through 60 will be a good strategy for some pupils. For example 40 minutes after 2.40 pm could be computed via 2.40 plus 20 minutes is 3.00 pm and thus to 3.20 pm.

There can be some confusion over am and pm. Try to pre-empt the difficulty (one possibility is simply alphabetical, a is before p) Also remember that a clock is now the only base 12 experience children will have. Days in a week is about the only good real life example of working with multiples of 7.

Index and Record of Use

Index and Record of Use continued

Name ....

Find the hidden numbers and signs

Fill in the missing signs in the sums below to make the answers correct:

2 5 = 10	18 2 = 9	21 9 = 12	14 5 = 9	19 11 = 8	4 10 = 40
56 9 = 8	23 8 = 31	11 4 = 44	13 7 = 20	45 2 = 47	34 12 = 46
45 9 = 36	90 8 = 98	45 9 = 5	90 10 = 9	7 8 = 56	45 19 = 64
6 6 = 36	23 23 = 46	13 3 = 39	88 13 = 75	49 4 = 53	21 19 = 40
60 6 = 10	17 9 = 26	34 22 = 12	56 4 = 52	77 11 = 7	14 7 = 21
41 2 = 82	67 23 = 90	42 7 = 6	11 56 = 67	21 7 = 28	55 15 = 70

Now colour all the boxes which are addition sums in red.

What number have you discovered?   ....

Now I am going to think of some numbers. See if you can work out the number I have in my head.

1.   I think of a number, double it, add 6 and I end up with 46.
     What was the number I started with?   ....

2.   If I start with 45 and divide it by 9, what must I do
     to get an answer of 15?   ....

3.   I think of a number, take away 25, divide by 5 and
     the answer is 15. What is the number I first thought of?...

4.   If I start with 78 and half it, what must I then do
     to get an answer of 28?   ....

Name ....

Number Stories

Choose 5 pairs of numbers from the following list and make up number stories to join them. Then work out the answers.

154	100	14	212	11	210	2

5	98	10	7	175	35	50	21

i.e.. Using 154 and 21. There were 154 marbles in a bag, if I added 21 more, how many would there be?
The answer is   154 + 21 = 175

1.   Using .... and ....

     The answer is ....

2.   Using ....and ....

     The answer is ....

3.   Using ....and ....

     The answer is ....

4.   Using................... and ....

     The answer is ....

5.   Using ....and ....

     The answer is ....

Checking Additions

$7 + 9 + 3 + 4 + 8 + 6 + 2 = ?$

Method 1
Adding the numbers in
order downwards

```
7  |
9  |   =16
3  ↓   19
4      23
8      31
6      37
2      39
39
```

Method 2
Adding the numbers in
order upwards

```
7      39
9      37
3      31
4      23
8  ↑   19
6  |   16
2  |  = 8
39
```

Method 3
Adding the numbers in
order downwards in pairs

```
7 ←
9 ──────→  9
3 ←        =10
4 ←
8 ←
6 ←        =10
2 ←        =10
39         39
```

Method 4
Adding the numbers in
order upwards in pairs

```
7 ←    =16 ←
9 ←               =23
3 ←    = 7 ←
4 ←
8 ←    =14 ←
6 ←               =16
2 →        2 ←
39                39
```

Use each of the 4 methods shown above to find the answers to

1. $5 + 4 + 7 + 3 + 1 + 5 + 6$

2. $8 + 4 + 4 + 7 + 2 + 1 + 6$

3. $5 + 8 + 3 + 3 + 9 + 5 + 2$

4. $7 + 5 + 6 + 3 + 2 + 4 + 8$

5. $9 + 6 + 3 + 4 + 1 + 5 + 2$

Name ....

Checking Calculations

The answer to a sum can be checked by doing a different sum with the same numbers

For example 16 + 37 = 53   can be checked by   53 - 37 = 16

Here are some more sums whose answers are to be checked.
Write down another sum which can be used to check that the answer is correct.
Use your calculator to check the answers of both sums and put a tick in the space provided if they are both right.

Sum	Sum for checking	Check
1. 84 + 79 = 163	....	....
2. 23 x 18 = 414	....	....
3. 502 - 287 = 215	....	....
4. 264 + 858 = 1122	....	....
5. 522 ÷ 58 = 9	....	....
6. 26 x 26 = 676	....	....
7. a half of 76 = 38	....	....
8. 322 - 59 = 263	....	....
9. a third of 135 = 45	....	....
10. 12 x 86 = 1032	....	....
11. 918 ÷ 34 = 27	....	....
12. a quarter of 252 = 63	....	....

4

Name ....

Number Stories

This is a 'number story'

There are ten pieces of super mint, sugar free, extra chewy gum in a packet.
If Mike buys six packets he gets sixty pieces.

This 'translates' to   10 x 6 = 60

Make up number stories for these statements.

1.   13 x 7 = 91

....

....

2.   £4.50 + £5.50 = £10.00

....

....

3.   103 - 44 = 59

....

....

4.   40 ÷ 5 = 8

....

....

5.   5 x £1.99 = £9.95

....

....

Name ....

Number Stories

Write a number story for each of the following sums.

1.   34 + 9 = 43

   ....

   ....

2.   6 x 8 = 48

   ....

   ....

3.   60 ÷ 5 = 12

   ....

   ....

4.   17 + 14 = 31

   ....

   ....

5.   25 - 18 = 7

   ....

   ....

6.   12 x 20 = 240

   ....

   ....

7.   245 - 126 = 119

   ....

   ....

Name ....

Are your results odd or even?

1. Choose 2 pairs of odd numbers and add them together.

    Are the results always odd or even?   ....

2. Now choose 2 groups of 3 odd numbers and add them together.

    Are the results always odd or even?   ....

    Why do you think this is?   ....

3. Choose 2 pairs of even numbers and add them together

    Are the results always odd or even?   ....

4. Now choose 2 groups of 3 even numbers and add them together.

    Are the results always odd or even?   ....

    Why do you think this is?   ....

5. What happens if you add an odd to an even number?

    Is the answer odd or even?   ....

    Do you think it will always be the same and why?   ....

6. Now try finding the difference between

    a)   2 odd numbers: ....

    b)   2 even numbers: ....

    c)   1 odd and 1 even number: ....

    Do you think your answers will always be the same, and why?.......................

    ....

Name ....

Check by reversing

You can check the sum 35 + 27 = 62 by doing 62 - 27. The answer should be 35.

Check these sums by doing the reverse sum.
Write down the sum you do and what the correct answer should be for those that are wrong.

	Check	**Correct answer**
1. 79 + 45 = 124	....	....
2. 89 - 34 = 54	....	....
3. 42 x 4 = 168	....	....
4. 56 + 231 = 297	....	....
5. 110 ÷ 2 = 210	....	....
6. 66 x 10 = 606	....	....
7. 135 - 98 = 37	....	....
8. 1236 ÷ 3 = 413	....	....

If you have a list of numbers to add together you can check by doing the list in reverse order.
i.e. 23 + 5 + 7 + 1 + 12 + 33 = 81   Can be checked by doing:
        33 + 12 + 1 + 7 + 5 + 23 = 81

Find the totals of these numbers and check by doing it again in reverse order.

1. 3 + 7 + 5 + 9 + 8 + 4 + 16 = ...

2. 29 + 15 + 7 + 5 + 12+ 3 + 6 = ...

3. 140 + 30 + 20 + 12 + 2 + 1 + 10 = ...

Name ....

Approximation & Estimation

By approximating the numbers in the following sums and then writing down a sum that you can do in your head find an estimate for the answer to the sum. Then work out the sum on a calculator to see how close your estimate is to the actual answer.

For example

Sum	Estimated Answer	Actual Answer
53 + 79	50 + 80 = 130	132

	Sum	Estimated Answer	Actual Answer
1.	84 + 58	....	....
2.	92 - 33	....	....
3.	394 + 117	....	....
4.	612 - 398	....	....
5.	17.2 + 5.7	....	....
6.	36.3 - 12.9	....	....
7.	3.9 x 2.2	....	....
8.	8.3 x 4.8	....	....
9.	16.4 x 9.7	....	....
10.	984.2 + 417.8	....	....
11.	490.1 - 293.9	....	....
12.	9.9 x 9.9	....	....

Name ....

Rounding and Estimating

Round (up or down) the numbers, then work out the estimate, for example

555 - 199 rounds to 555 - 200   (or 550 - 200) then work out as

555 - 200 = 355   (or 550 - 200 = 350)

1.   699 + 195 = ... + ... = ...

2.   587 x 9 = ... x.................. =..................

3.   579 ÷ 19 =.................. ÷ .... =..................

4.   388 - 202 = ... - .... = ...

5.   95 + 156 = ... + ... = ...

6.   99p x 8 = ... x .... = ...

7.   £499 - £211 =.................. - .... = ...

8.   139 ÷ 48 =.................. ÷ .... = ...

9.   248 + 353 = ... + ... = ...

10. 753 - 447 = ... - .... = ...

Name ....

Missing Operations

Put the correct sign in each of the following sums

1.   8 .... 2 = 16   2.   10 ..... 3 = 7

3.   24 ..... 2 = 12   4.   6 ..... 4 = 2

5.   9 ..... 3 = 12   6.   20 ..... 5 = 4

7.   15 ..... 5 = 10   8.   4 ..... 4 = 16

9.   6 ..... 10 = 16   10.   40 ..... 8 = 5

11.   8 ..... 8 = 1   12.   6 ..... 2 = 3

13.   18 ..... 12 = 30   14.   25 ..... 2 = 50

15.   4 ..... 4 = 8   16.   12 ..... 3 = 9

17.   36 ..... 6 = 6   18.   30 ..... 10 = 3

19.   3 ..... 2 = 5   20.   24 ..... 3 = 8

21.   16 ..... 2 = 14   22.   14 ..... 2 = 28

23.   8 ..... 2 = 4   24.   6 ..... 6 = 12

Patterns with the Calculator

Work out the answers to these sums using your calculator. Try to use the patterns to predict the answers.

Pattern 1

$$1 \times 9 \quad + \quad 1 = 10$$
$$12 \times 9 \quad + \quad 2 = \text{.....................................}$$
$$123 \times 9 \quad + \quad 3 = \text{.....................................}$$
$$1234 \times 9 \quad + \quad 4 = \text{.....................................}$$
$$12345 \times 9 \quad + \quad 5 = \text{.....................................}$$

Pattern 2

$$1 \times 8 \quad + \quad 1 = \text{.....................................}$$
$$12 \times 8 \quad + \quad 2 = \text{.....................................}$$
$$123 \times 8 \quad + \quad 3 = \text{.....................................}$$
$$1234 \times 8 \quad + \quad 4 = \text{.....................................}$$
$$12345 \times 8 \quad + \quad 5 = \text{.....................................}$$

Pattern 3

$$1 \times 1 \quad = \text{..........................}$$
$$11 \times 11 \quad = \text{..........................}$$
$$111 \times 111 \quad = \text{..........................}$$
$$1111 \times 1111 \quad = \text{..........................}$$
$$11111 \times 11111 \quad = \text{..........................}$$

Pattern 4

$$1 \times 9109 \quad = \text{..........................}$$
$$2 \times 9109 \quad = \text{..........................}$$
$$3 \times 9109 \quad = \text{..........................}$$
$$4 \times 9109 \quad = \text{..........................}$$
$$5 \times 9109 \quad = \text{..........................}$$

Name ....

Calculator Words

Work out each sum on your calculator. Turn the calculator upside down and read the word on the screen. Write the word as your answer.

1.   1062 x 5 add 7   ....

2.   32312 ÷ 4   ....

3.   530 x 7 minus 5   ....

4.   1377 x 4   ....

5.   500 x 70 plus 7   ....

6.   1234 + 4104   ....

7.   100 000 - 42 265   ....

8.   4 765 650 ÷ 15 plus 8   ....

9.   4500 - 102 divide by 6   ....

10.   3943275 ÷ 555   ....

Calculators and Checking

Use you calculator to work out the reverse operation (for example check a subtraction by adding) and check if the given answer is correct.

1.   584 - 96 = 488   check by   488 + 96 = ...   ✔ ✘

2.   907 - 158 - 759   check by   759 + 158 = ...   ✔ ✘

3.   225 ÷ 5 = 51   check by   51 x 5 = ...   ✔ ✘

4.   876 + 765 = 1641   check by   1641 - 765 = ...   ✔ ✘

5.   11325 ÷ 25 = 453   check by   453 x 25 = ...   ✔ ✘

6.   89 x 42 = 3838   check by   3838 ÷ 42 = ...   ✔ ✘

7.   1001- 444 = 557   check by   557 + 444 = ...   ✔ ✘

8.   51 x 49 = 2499   check by   2499 ÷ 49 = ...   ✔ ✘

9.   955 + 655 = 1600   check by   1600 - 655=   ....   ✔ ✘

10.   101 x 22 = 2222   check by   2222 ÷ 22 = ...   ✔ ✘

Name ....

Russian Multiplication

In the 19th century, peasants in a poor part of Russia discovered an easier way of multiplying numbers. This is how it works:-

To multiply 17 x 15

Halve the number in this column, and ignore the remainder		Double the number in this column
17	x	15
~~8~~	~~x~~	~~30~~
~~4~~	~~x~~	~~60~~
~~2~~	~~x~~	~~120~~
1	x	240
		255

Cross out all the rows which have an even number in the first column. Add up all the numbers left in the second column.

Use the Russian method to do these examples.

1.   21 x 25

....

2.   19 x 15

....

3.   23 x 35

....

4.   21 x 32

....

5.   19 x 21

....

6.   27 x 41

....

Check your answers with a calculator

Wrong Answers

In each of the sums below the answer is wrong.
Without doing the sum in your head, on paper or on a calculator give a reason why the answer is wrong.

1. 392 + 279 = 571

    ....

    ....

2. 15 x 12 = 140

    ....

    ....

3. 563 - 247 = 810

    ....

    ....

4. 372 ÷ 5 = 76

    ....

    ....

5. 24 + 58 + 46 + 78 + 32 = 233

    ....

    ....

6. 56 x 6 x 10 = 3356

    ....

    ....

7. 1545 ÷ 2 = 774

    ....

    ....

Name ....

Money - Change

1) Find the correct change from **£1** when you buy

    a)   a newspaper costing 45p   ....

    b)   a bar of chocolate costing 32p   ....

    c)   3 stamps costing 20p each   ....

    d)   2 stamps costing 26p each   ....

2) Find the correct change from **£5** when buying

    a)   a magazine costing £1.50   ....

    b)   a box of chocolates costing £3.80   ....

    c)   2 bottles of lemonade costing £1.30 each   ....

3) Find the change from **£10** when buying

    a)   a CD costing £7.50   ....

    b)   a book costing £5.95   ....

    c)   a football scarf costing £8.99   ....

Name ....

Money Problems

1. Amanda saves 60p a week.
    How much does she save in 8 weeks ?   ....

2. How many 20p stamps can you buy for £5 ?   ....

3. How much change do I get from £1 if I buy 2 bars
    of chocolate costing 34p each ?   ....

4. Write down the 4 coins which make 28p exactly. ....

5. Theatre tickets cost £7.50 for Adults and £5.50 for Children.
    Find the total cost of 2 Adult tickets and 3 Children tickets. ....

6. Cheese costs £5.38 per kg.
    Find the cost of $\frac{1}{2}$ kg of cheese.   ....

7. How many 26p stamps can you buy for £2 ?   ....

    How much change do you get ?   ....

8. Four people share the cost of a meal equally between them.
    The total cost was £53.80. How much does each of them
    have to pay ?   ....

9. Find the total cost of 7 paper-back books
    costing £4.69 each.   ....

10. I have 5 coins. None of them are £1 coins.
    Two of them are silver.
    What is the largest amount that I could have ? ....

    What is the smallest amount that I could have ? ....

11. When I go into a shop I have £17.62. When I come
    out I have £2.85. How much did I spend in the shop ? ....

12. Kirsty is sponsored 5p for each length she swims. She swims 40 lengths.

    How much does she raise from each sponsor ?   ....
    If she has 16 sponsors then how much does
    she raise altogether ?   ....

Problems

1. There are 5 shelves in a bookcase and 8 books on each shelf.
    How many books are there altogether in the bookcase? ....

2. A milkman delivers 4 bottles of milk to a house on every
    day of the week except Sunday.
    How many bottles of milk are delivered?   ....

3. Find the total cost of 6 books which cost £7 each.   ....

4. A worker earns £4 an hour. How much will the worker
    be paid for 9 hours work?   ....

5. If a person cycles at 12 miles per hour then how far
    would they go if they cycled for 5 hours?   ....

6. If each coach has 30 seats then how many seats are
    there altogether in 6 coaches?   ....

7. If a person is paid £3 an hour then how much would
    they earn if they worked for 18 hours?   ....

8. Find the total cost of 8 stamps costing 26p each.   ....

9. In a small theatre there are 16 rows of seats and
    9 seats in each row. How many seats are there
    altogether in the theatre?   ....

10. How many days are there in 15 weeks?   ....

11. If a cream cake costs 45p then how much would
    8 cream cakes cost?   ....

12. There are 14 pounds in a stone. How many pounds
    are there in 9 stone?   ....

Name ....

Money

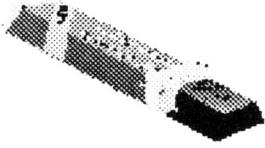

Mars 35p

Topic 32p

Kit-Kat 28p

Crunchie 30p

Aero 27p

Find the cost of

1. 1 Mars and 1 Kit-Kat   ....

2. 2 Aeros   ....

3. 1 Topic, 1 Crunchie and 1 Aero   ....

4. 3 Topics   ....

5. 1 Kit-Kat and 1 Topic   ....

6. 2 Kit-Kats   ....

7. 2 Mars and 1 Crunchie   ....

8. 2 Crunchies and 1 Aero   ....

9. 2 Topics, 1 Areo and 2 Mars   ....

10. 4 Crunchies and 3 Mars   ....

Name ....

Money - Drinks

Cola 65p

Milk Shake 75p

Wine 95p

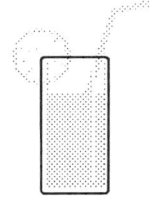
Orange 55p

Coffee 85p

1. Find the cost of

   a)   2 milk shakes ....

   b)   1 Cola and 1 coffee ....

   c)   1 glass of wine and 2 oranges ....

   d)   1 milk shake, 2 Colas and 3 oranges ....

2. How much change do I get from £2 if I buy
   a)   1 glass of wine ....

   b)   1 orange and 1 milk shake ....

   c)   2 coffees ....

3. How much change do I get from £5 if I buy
   a)   4 milk shakes ....

   b)   5 glasses of wine ....

   c)   1 of each of the five drinks on sale ....

Name ....

Money - Change

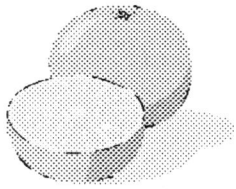

Oranges 19p each

Peaches 27peach

Melons 89p each

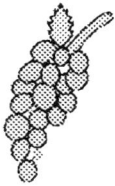

Grapes 75p per bag

Cherries 95p per bag

Sweet Corn 32p each

Find the correct change from **£1** when you buy

1.   a bag of grapes   ....

2.   a melon   ....

3.   a peach   ....

4.   a sweet corn   ....

5.   a bag of cherries   ....

6.   an orange   ....

7.   2 peaches   ....

8.   5 oranges   ....

9.   a bag of grapes and an orange   ....

Name ....

Money - Change

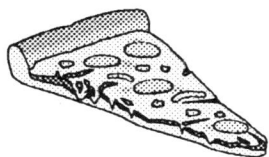

Pizza Slice 63p

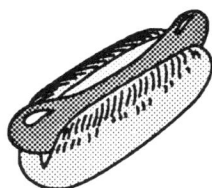

Hot Dog £1.25

Hamburger £1.55

Chocolate Biscuits
55p

Ice Cream 85p

Ice Lolly 45p

Find the correct change from **£2** when you buy

1. a hot dog   ....

2. a hamburger   ....

3. 2 slices of pizza   ....

4. an ice cream and an ice lolly   ....

5. a hot dog and chocolate biscuits ....

6. a hamburger and an ice lolly   ....

7. a slice of pizza and a hot dog   ....

8. 2 ice creams   ....

9. 4 ice lollies   ....

33

Name ....

Investigate

1. Half way between 20 and 30 is?   ....
    Half way between 50 and 100 is?   ....
    What is special about the numbers half way between any
    multiples of ten? Try some more if you don't know yet. ....
    ....
    ....

2. Draw on the lines of symmetry on these regular polygons.

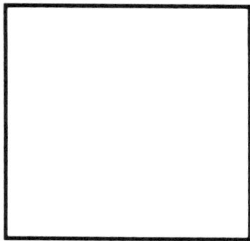

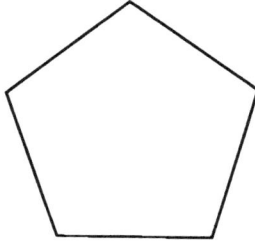

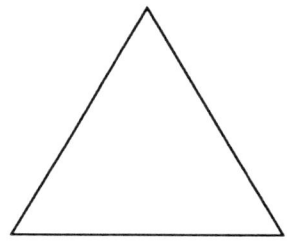

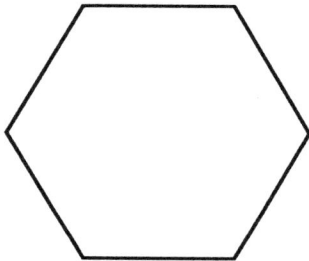

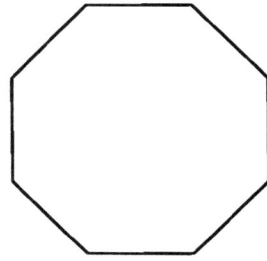

    What do you notice about the number of lines of symmetry compared with
    the number of sides of each shape? ....
    ....

3. The perimeter of this rectangle is $10 + 4 + 10 + 4 = 28$ cm

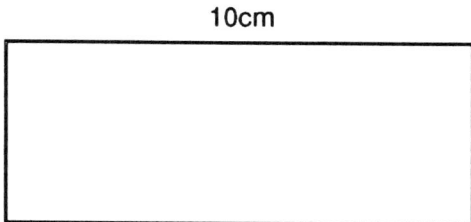

    10cm

    4cm   What other sum could you do using
              different signs to get the answer 28?

              ....
    Draw another rectangle and write down 2 ways of working out the perimeter.

34

Name ....

Rules and Sequences

1. How many days are there in 8 weeks?   ....
    Write down the calculation you used to work out that sum.

    ....

    Explain how you could work out the number of days in any number of weeks.

    ....

    ....

2.

    15cm

    6cm

    8cm

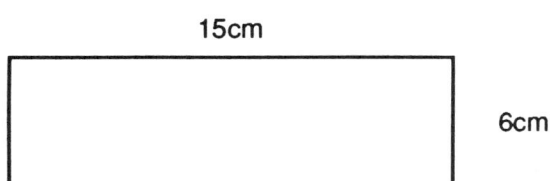

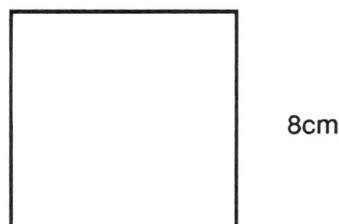

    What is the perimeter of the rectangle?   ....
    Explain how you worked out that sum.

    ....

    What is the perimeter of the square?   ....
    Explain how you worked out that sum.

    ....

3. Follow the rules to write down the next six numbers in each of these
    sequences.

	Rule	First number					
a)	Add 3	2	....	....	....	....	....
b)	Take 2	40	....	....	....	....	....
c)	Add 5	3	....	....	....	....	....

4. Explain the rule for these sequences:

    a) 30, 26, 22, 18, 14. ....

    b) 5, 11, 17, 23, 29 ....

35

Puzzles

Use the grid below to answer the following questions:

13	37	16	89
40	2	4	10
5	600	24	30
14	102	20	19

1. Find a pair of numbers which will give you one answer in the grid when they are added together and another when they are multiplied together. Colour these 4 numbers green.

   Write down the 2 sums here: ....
   ....

2. Find 2 numbers in the grid which will give a difference that is also shown in the grid. Colour these 3 numbers red.

   Write down the sum here: ....

3. Using only numbers in the grid, find 1 number which will divide into another one to give you an answer that is also in the grid. Colour these 3 numbers blue.

   Write down the sum here: ....
   Using the numbers: 1, 2, 4, and 10 and + and -, see if you can make all the numbers from 1 to 17.

1. = ...
2. = ...
3. = ...
4. = ...
5. = ...
6. = ...
7. = ...
8. = ...
9. = ...
10. = ...
11. = 10 + 1
12. = ...
13. = ...
14. = ...
15. = ...
16. = ...
17. = ...

Name ....

How did you do that?

16 x 3   This is 10 x 3 = 30 and 6 x 3 = 18. So the answer is 48

You try using a similar method to explain how to work out these sums and find the answers.

1.   17 x 2   ....

2.   23 x 7   ....

3.   51 x 3   ....

4.   8 x 15   ....

For 59 + 34   I could say: 60 + 34 = 94, but I need 1 less = 93

For 304 - 196   I could say: I need 4 more to make 200 and 100 more to make 300 and then 4 more to make 304. So I need 108.

For 45 ÷ 2   I could say $\frac{1}{2}$ of 40 is 20 and $\frac{1}{2}$ of 5 is 2.5 so the answer is 22.5

Try these sums explaining as you go along how you get the answer.

1.   39 + 74   ....

2.   802 - 354   ....

3.   912 - 788   ....

4.   34 + 56   ....

5.   400 - 105   ....

6   73 ÷ 2   ....

7.   99 ÷ 2   ....

8.   195 + 202   ....

Name ....

Number Triangles

The table shows the number of 'number rows' in each triangle and the sum of the numbers around the perimeter (outer numbers) for each triangle.

Find the pattern and fill in the last three spaces.

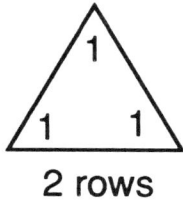

2 rows

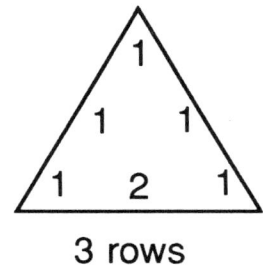

3 rows

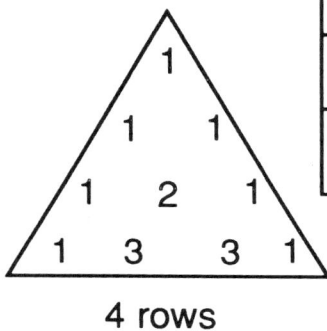

4 rows

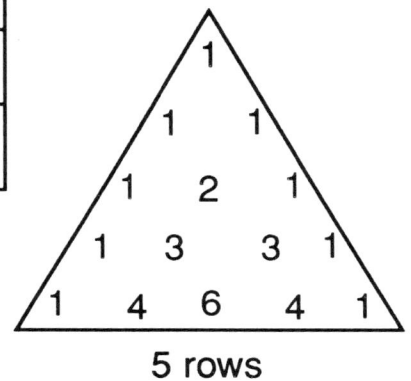

5 rows

Number of rows	Sum of numbers Around the perimeter
2	3
3	7
4	13
5	23
6	....
7	....
8	....

Draw number triangles with

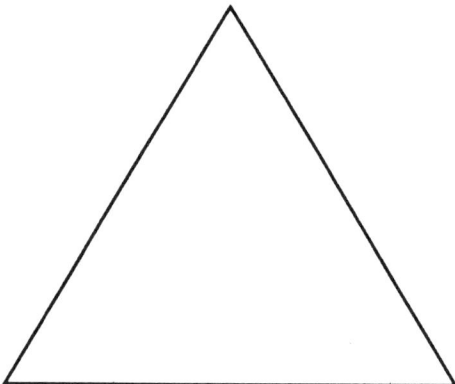

6 rows

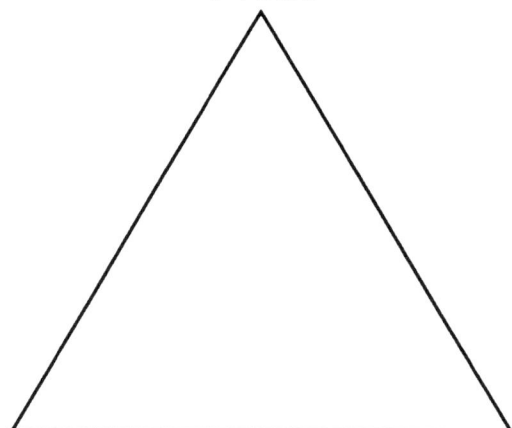

7 rows

38

Name ....

In every

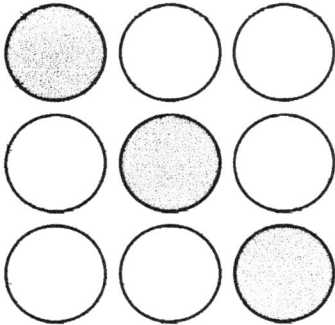

In the top row 1 in every 3 circles is grey.

In the top two rows 2 in every 6 circles are grey.

In the whole pattern 3 in every 9 circles are grey.

1. If the pattern had 12 circles, how many would be grey? ....

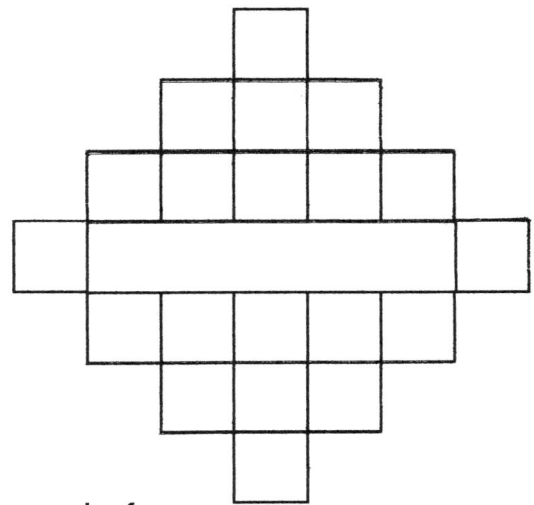

2. Shade in 1 in every 4 squares in this pattern.

3. For every 5 drinks of cola I buy I get an extra cola free. If I buy 15 colas, how many extra colas do I get free? ....

4. For every 4 plain tiles used on the kitchen wall there is 1 tile with a pattern. If there are 40 plain tiles, how many patterned tiles are there on the wall?   ....

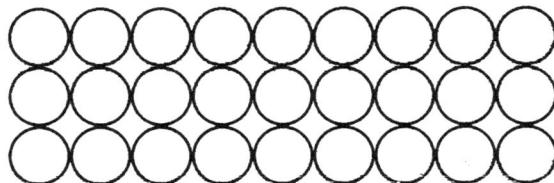

5. Shade in 2 in every 3 circles.

6. For every 5 apple trees in an orchard there is 1 cherry tree. If there are 5 cherry trees, how many apple trees are there? ....

7. Keval has to save 6 tokens for every model he is collecting. If he has 36 tokens, how many models can he get? ....

Finding missing numbers in sums

Working

1. 23 x .... = 230

2. 280 ÷ .... = 28

3.
```
        2 .....
    x     3
      ———————
      6   9
```

4.
```
        1 ... 4
    x       2
      ———————
      2 6 8
```

5.
```
        6 .....
    x       4
      ———————
      2 5 2
```

6.
```
      ...... 6 3
      x       2
        ———————
        5 2 6
```

7.
```
        2 1........
    10) 2 1 4 0
```

8. 23 x .... = 460

Number Machines

Imagine putting these numbers into this machine. What would come out the other side?

20   ....

16   ....

25   ....

33   x 2 + 3   ....

15   ....

37   ....

Now design a number machine of your own

Decision Diagram

You have a 1p , 2p , 5p , 10p , 20p, 50p and £1 coin.
Use the diagram below to find which coin goes into which box.

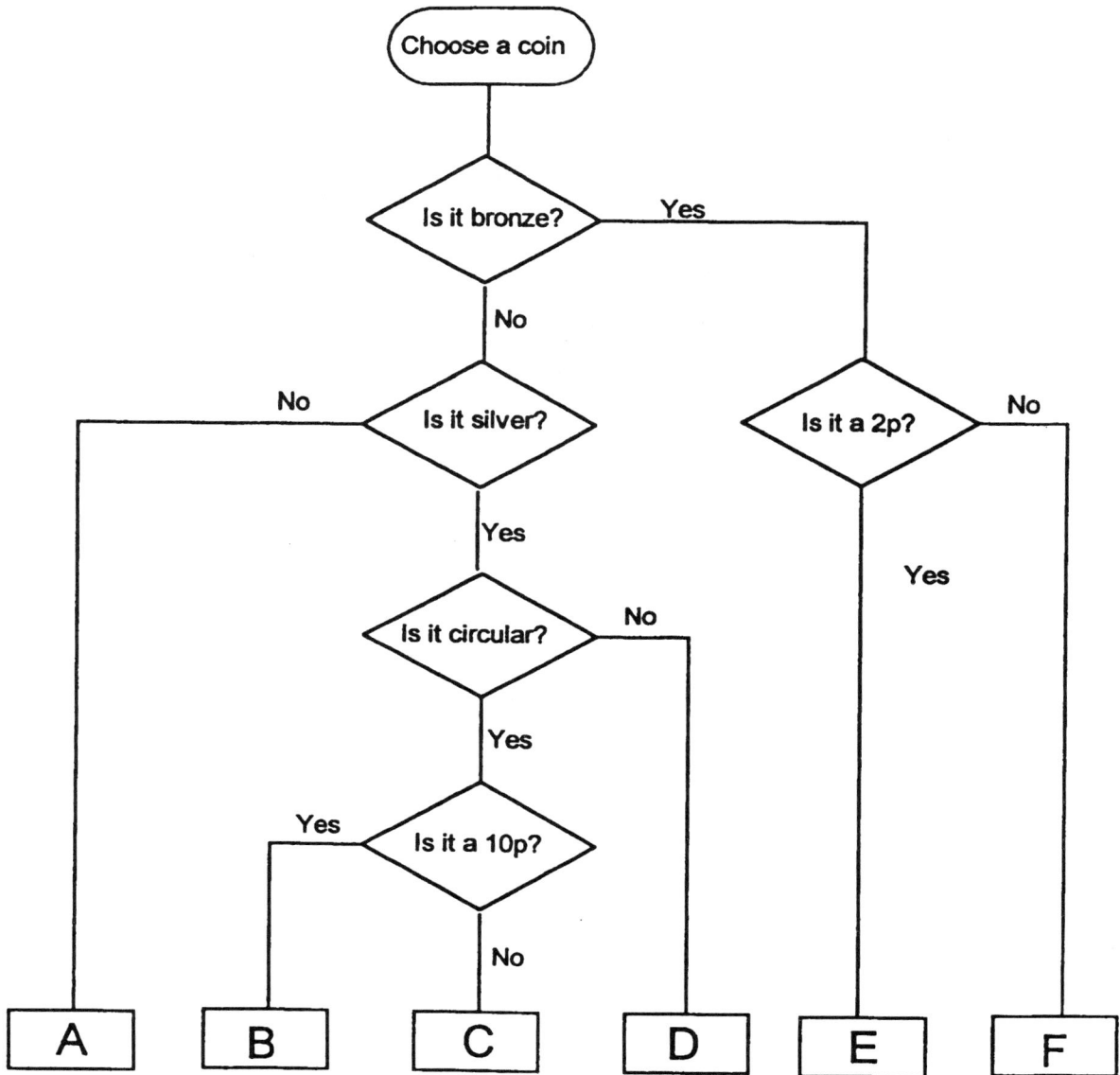

```
                        ┌─────────────────┐
                        │  Choose a coin  │
                        └────────┬────────┘
                                 │
                            ◇ Is it bronze? ◇ ──── Yes ────┐
                                 │                         │
                                 No                        │
                                 │                         │
        No ──── ◇ Is it silver? ◇        ◇ Is it a 2p? ◇ ──── No ──┐
        │              │                         │                 │
        │             Yes                       Yes                │
        │              │                         │                 │
        │     ◇ Is it circular? ◇ ── No ──┐      │                 │
        │              │                  │      │                 │
        │             Yes                 │      │                 │
        │              │                  │      │                 │
        │   Yes ── ◇ Is it a 10p? ◇       │      │                 │
        │    │          │                 │      │                 │
        │    │         No                 │      │                 │
   ┌────┴┐ ┌─┴─┐ ┌─────┴┐ ┌──────┐ ┌──────┐ ┌────┴─┐
   │  A  │ │ B │ │  C   │ │  D   │ │  E   │ │  F   │
   └─────┘ └───┘ └──────┘ └──────┘ └──────┘ └──────┘
```

Write your answers here

Box A   ....   Box B   ....

Box C   ....   Box D   ....

Box E   ....   Box F   ....

Equations

Find the numbers that go on the lines to fit these equations

1. $4 + \dots = 12$

2. $8 + \dots = 15$

3. $10 - \dots = 4$

4. $\dots + 7 = 20$

5. $\dots - 7 = 5$

6. $13 + \dots = 25$

7. $\dots - 5 = 12$

8. $23 - \dots = 10$

9. $14 + \dots = 30$

10. $\dots - 17 = 5$

11. $3 \times \dots = 12$

12. $5 \times \dots = 15$

13. $\dots \times 2 = 14$

14. $20 \div \dots = 5$

15. $\dots \div 3 = 4$

16. $8 \times \dots = 80$

17. $\dots \times 3 = 9$

18. $\dots \div 6 = 2$

19. $12 \div \dots = 3$

20. $5 \times \dots = 40$

Mixed Arithmetic

1. Do each sum as quickly as you can and write the answer in the space provided.

   a) 4 + 7 = ...
   b) 8 - 2 = ...
   c) 10 - 3 = ...

   d) 4 x 2 = ...
   e) 8 + 9 = ...
   f) 20 - 5 = ...

   g) 3 x 5 = ...
   h) 11 - 8 = ...
   i) 12 + 5 = ...

   j) 10 - 2 = ...
   k) 7 + 6 = ...
   l) 2 x 9 = ...

   m) 13 - 8 = ...
   n) 14 - 2 = ...
   o) 15 + 8 = ...

2. Do each sum and show all of your working

   a)
   ```
     75
    +56
    ————
   ```

   b)
   ```
    234
    +67
    ————
   ```

   c)
   ```
     71
    -47
    ————
   ```

   d)
   ```
     61
     19
   +108
   ————
   ```

   e)
   ```
     35
    x 3
    ————
   ```

   f)
   ```
    203
    x 4
    ————
   ```

   g)
   ```
    402
   -167
   ————
   ```

   h)
   ```
    253
    x 2
    ————
   ```

   i)
   ```
     86
     43
    +74
    ————
   ```

   j)
   ```
    321
    x 5
    ————
   ```

   k)
   ```
    346
   +287
   ————
   ```

   l)
   ```
   2000
   -642
   ————
   ```

   m)
   ```
     41
    324
   + 77
   ————
   ```

   n)
   ```
    830
    x 2
    ————
   ```

   o)
   ```
   1803
   -564
   ————
   ```

Name ....

Pascal's Triangle

Fill in the spaces with the missing numbers in the number pattern below.

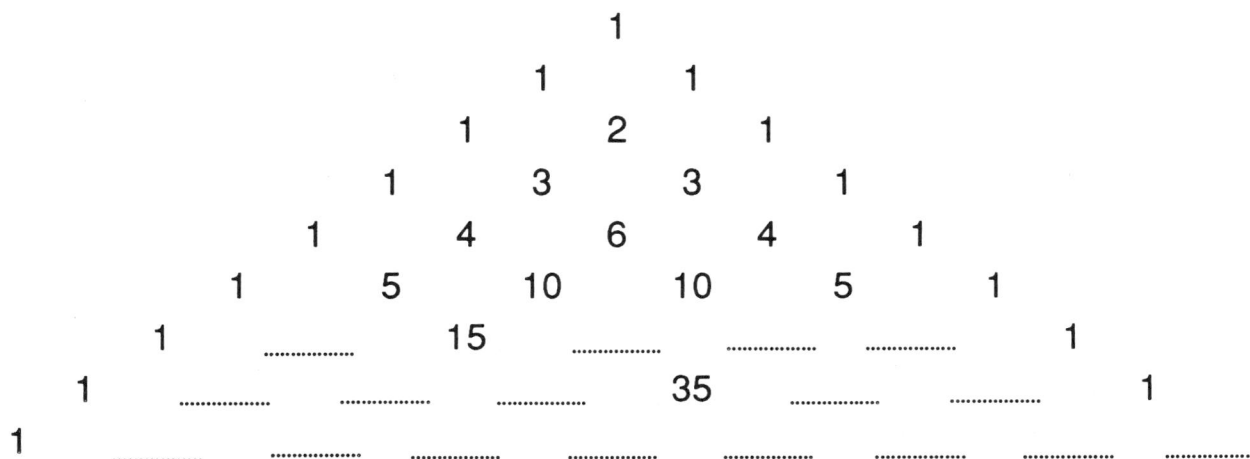

```
                              1
                          1       1
                      1       2       1
                  1       3       3       1
              1       4       6       4       1
          1       5      10      10       5       1
      1  ........    15   ........  ........  ........     1
   1  ........ ........ ........    35   ........ ........     1
1 ........ ........ ........ ........ ........ ........ ........ ........
```

Now add all the numbers in each row of Pascal's Triangle and write the answers in the table below.

Row 1	
Row 2	
Row 3	
Row 4	
Row 5	
Row 6	
Row 7	
Row 8	
Row 9	

What do you notice about the numbers in the right hand column?

....

....

Name ....

Matchstick Patterns

Complete the table to show how many matches are needed to make each of the matchstick patterns below.

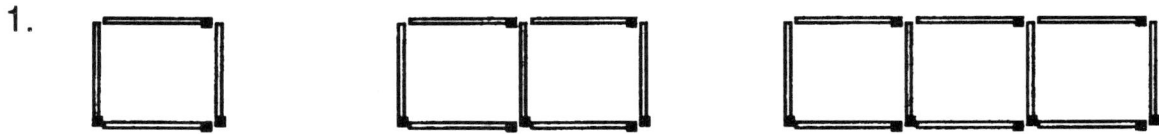

1.

Pattern 1   Pattern 2   Pattern 3

Pattern Number	1	2	3	4	5	6
Number of matchsticks						

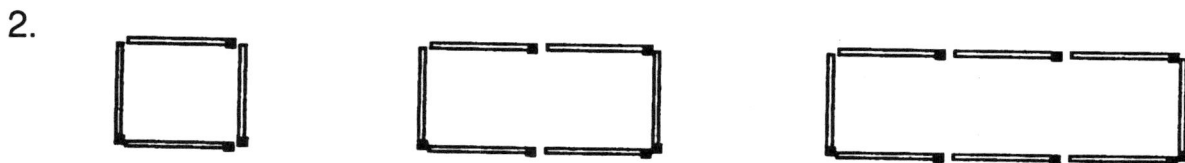

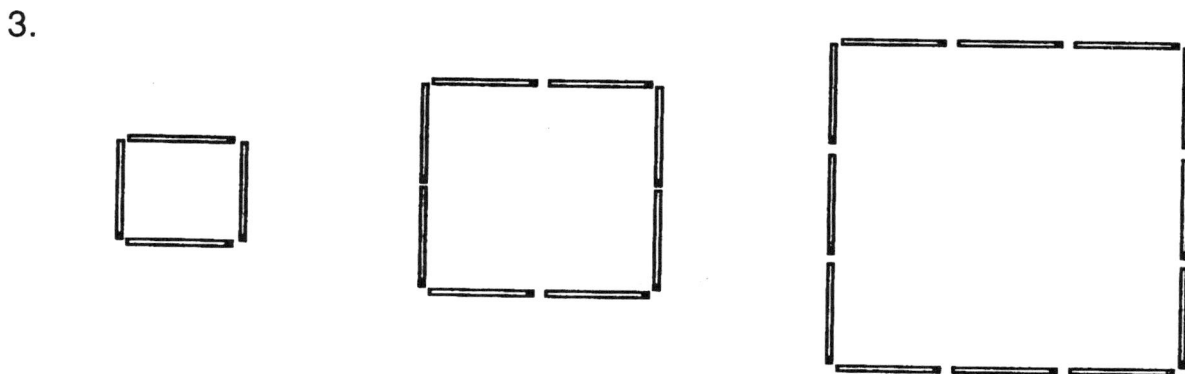

2.

Pattern 1   Pattern 2   Pattern 3

Pattern Number	1	2	3	4	5	6
Number of matchsticks						

3.

Pattern 1   Pattern 2   Pattern 3

Pattern Number	1	2	3	4	5	6
Number of matchsticks						

Shape Puzzle

Draw the 5 shapes shown below onto squared paper.
Cut them out and then put them together again to make a square.

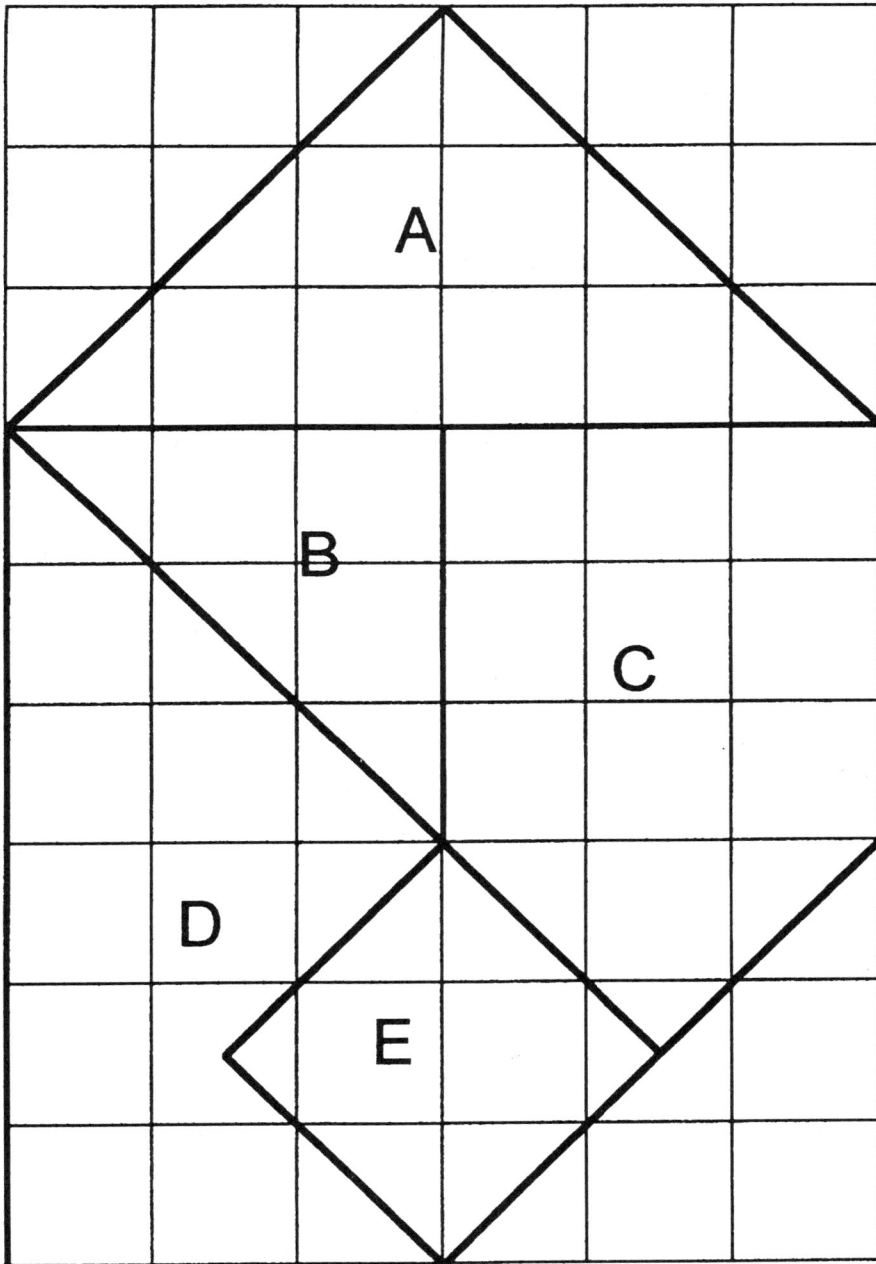

Name ....

Shape Puzzle

Show how to cut the shaded shape **A** into 2 pieces which can then be rearranged to make each of the shapes **B , C , D , E , F , G , H , I , J** and **K**.

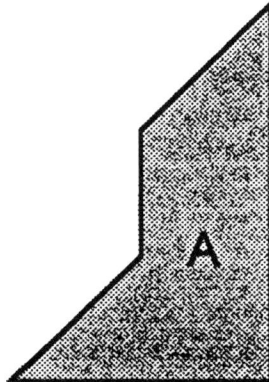

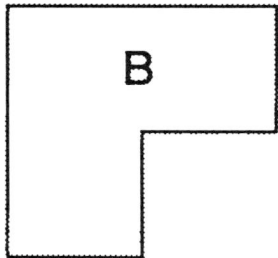

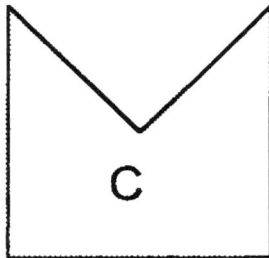

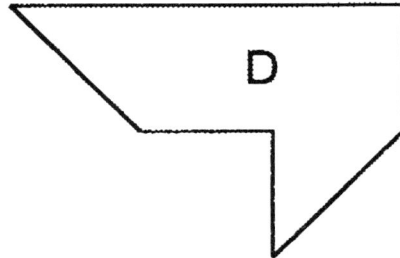

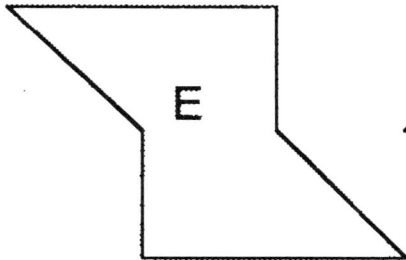

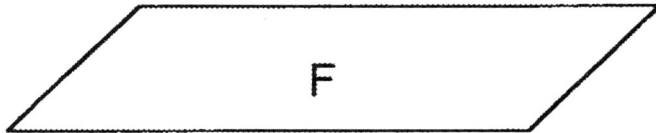

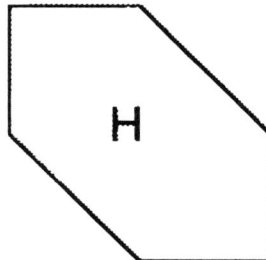

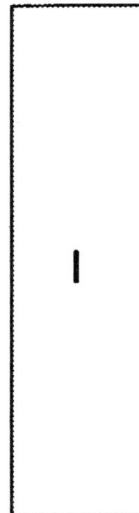

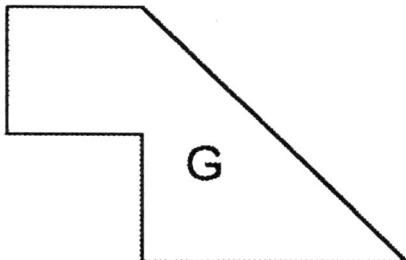

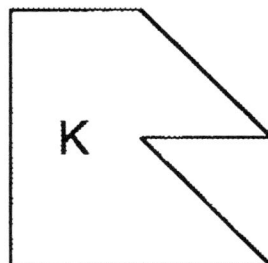

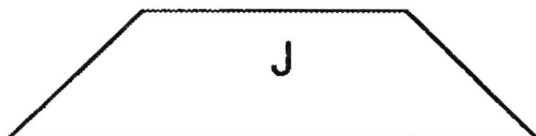

Shape Puzzles

1. How many squares are there altogether in the diagram?

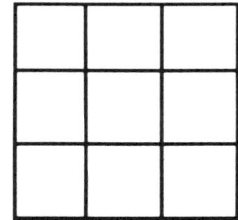

   ....

2. How many triangles are there altogether in the diagram?

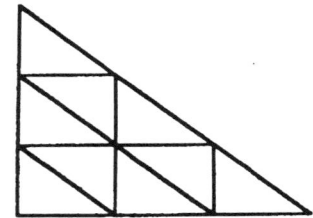

   ....

3. The length of the edge of the big cube is 3 times the length of the edge of the small cube. How many small cubes will fit into the big cube?

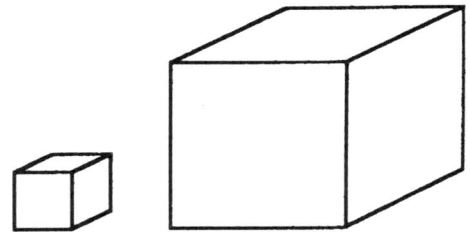

   ....

4. The diagram shows a pentagon. How many diagonals does it have?

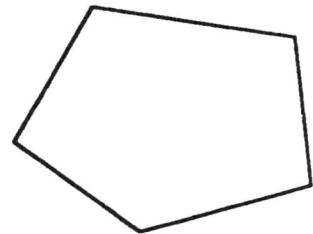

   ....

5. Complete the pattern below.

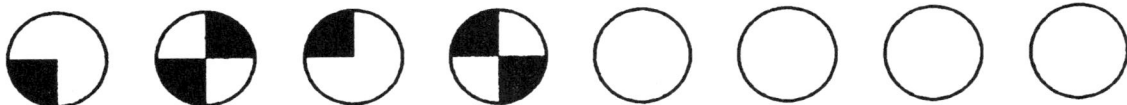

Number Puzzles

1. Write the numbers 1, 2, 3, 4, 5, 6, 7, 8 in the circles so that the sum of the numbers in each of the 4 lines of the square is the same.

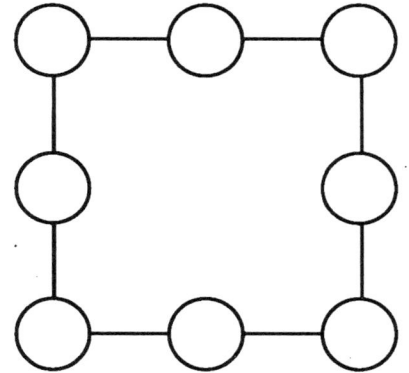

2. If $\triangle$ + $\square$ = $\cap$ and $\square$ + $\square$ = $\triangle$

   and $\cap$ = 6 then find the values of $\triangle$ and $\square$

3. Write the numbers 1, 2, 3, 4, 5, 6 in the circles so that the sum of the numbers in each of the 3 lines of the triangle is the same.

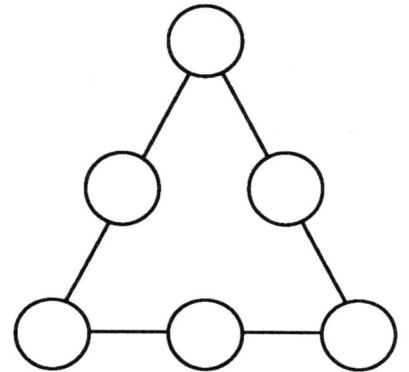

4. Write the same number in each of the circles so that the sum is correct.

   $\bigcirc$ x $\bigcirc$ + $\bigcirc$ = 30

5. Find the missing numbers in the following sums.

   a)
   ```
       4?
     + ?7
     ----
       92
   ```

   b)
   ```
       ?1
     - 2?
     ----
       46
   ```

6. Write the same number in each of the circles so that the sum is correct.

   $\bigcirc$ x $\bigcirc$ - $\bigcirc$ = 42

Name ....

Function Machines

Fill in the missing numbers in the following function machines.

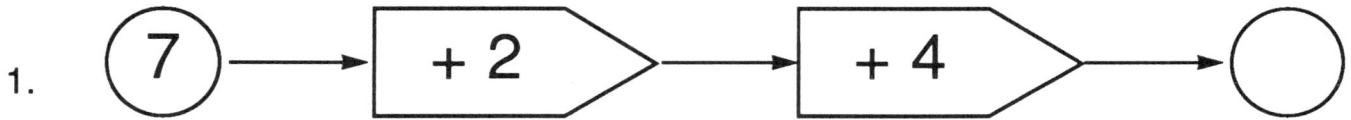

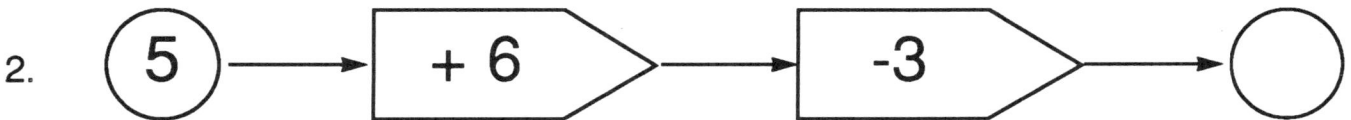

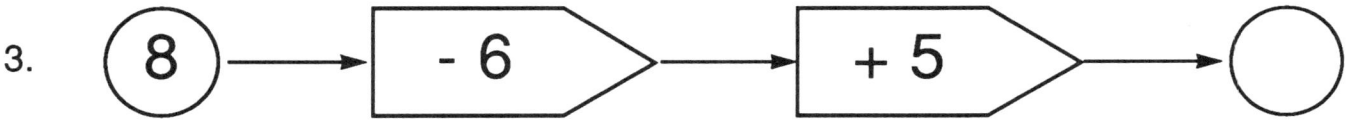

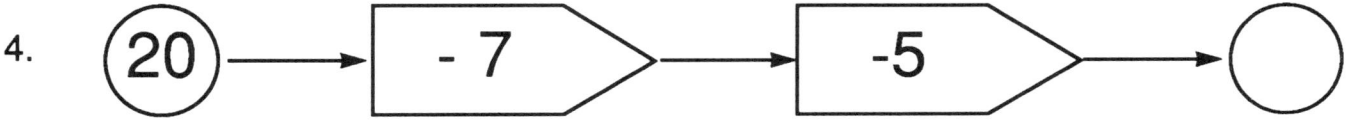

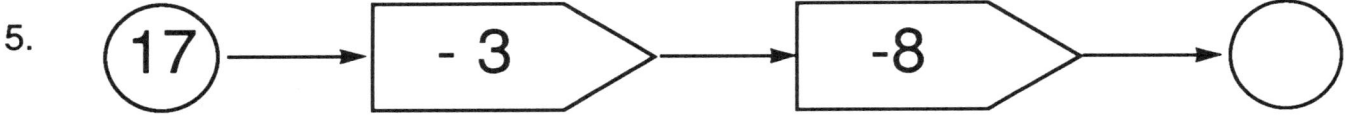

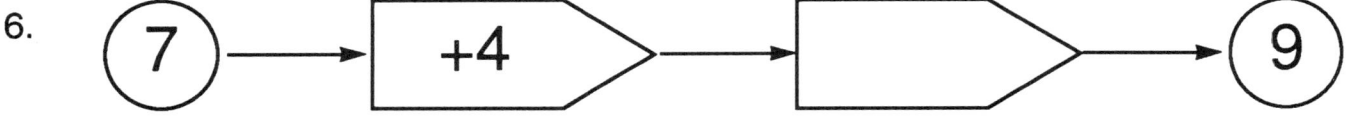

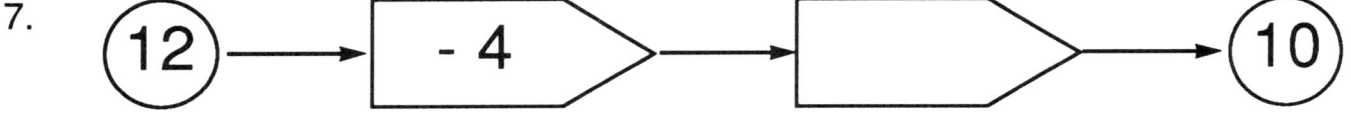

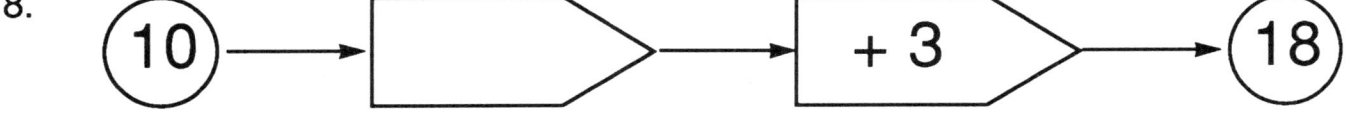

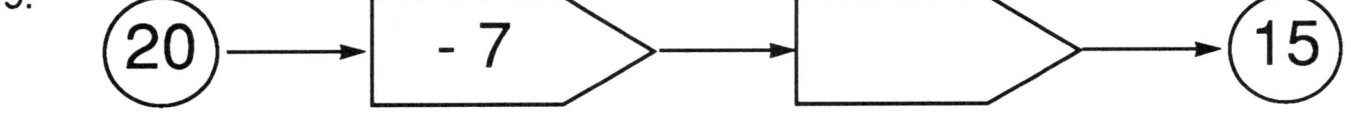

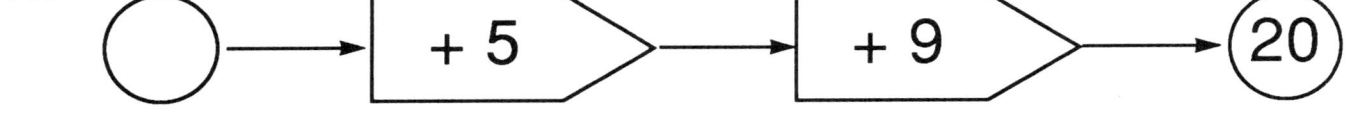

1. (7) → | + 2 | → | + 4 | → ( )

2. (5) → | + 6 | → | -3 | → ( )

3. (8) → | - 6 | → | + 5 | → ( )

4. (20) → | - 7 | → | -5 | → ( )

5. (17) → | - 3 | → | -8 | → ( )

6. (7) → | +4 | → | | → (9)

7. (12) → | - 4 | → | | → (10)

8. (10) → | | → | + 3 | → (18)

9. (20) → | - 7 | → | | → (15)

10. ( ) → | + 5 | → | + 9 | → (20)

Input/Output Devices

Fill in the missing numbers in the following input/output devices.

1. (8) → | + 5 | → ◯

2. (12) → | - 7 | → ◯

3. (5) → | x 3 | → ◯

4. (14) → | ÷ 2 | → ◯

5. (20) → | - 11 | → ◯

6. (20) → | ÷ 5 | → ◯

7. ◯ → | - 4 | → (9)

8. ◯ → | x 2 | → (18)

9. ◯ → | + 8 | → (14)

10. ◯ → | ÷ 4 | → (4)

Crossnumber

Across

1. $30 - 13 =$
2. $18 \div 2 =$
6. $6 \times 6 =$
7. $5 \times 10 =$
10. $35 \div 5 =$
11. $9 \times 9 =$
12. $6 \times 3 =$
13. $12 \div 3 =$
14. $8 \times 8 =$
18. $27 + 18 =$
19. $12 \div 4 =$
20. $3 \times 8 =$

Down

1. $64 + 36 =$
3. $4 \times 4 =$
4. $4 \times 7 =$
5. $5 \times 5 =$
8. $265 + 118 =$
9. $200 - 14 =$
15. $8 \times 5 =$
16. $500 - 146 =$
17. $48 \div 2 =$
18. $7 \times 7 =$

Name ....

Number Squares

Complete the number squares below

1.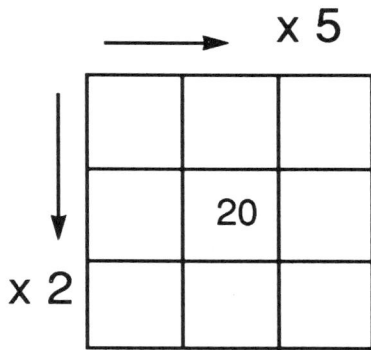

2.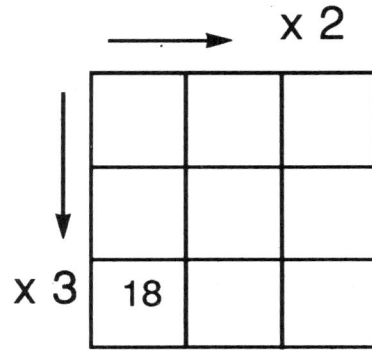

3.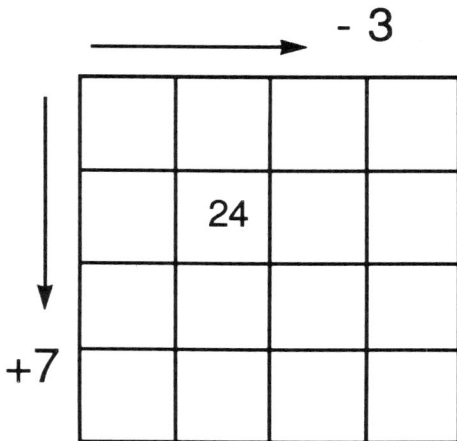

4.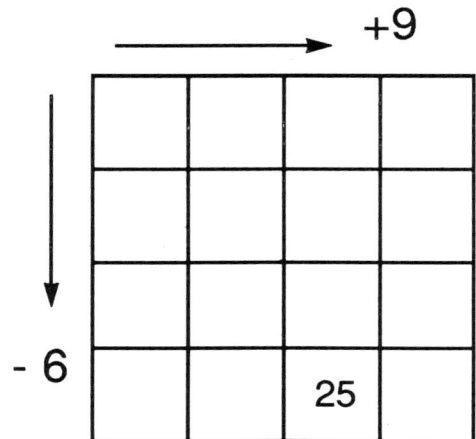